NO MORE FEAR

Also by Joseph Prince

Destined to Reign 15th Anniversary Edition

Expedition Promised Land

Hope That Never Fails

Give Me This Mountain

Unstoppable Faith

Eat Your Way to Life and Health

No More Mind Games

Anchored

Live the Let-Go Life

The Prayer of Protection

Grace Revolution

The Power of Right Believing

Unmerited Favor

Health and Wholeness Through the Holy Communion

Healing Promises

Provision Promises

For more information on these books and other inspiring resources, visit JosephPrince.com.

JOSEPH PRINCE

NO MORE FEAR

28 THOUGHTS TO LIVING A WORRY-FREE LIFE

No More Fear—28 Thoughts to Living a Worry-Free Life

ISBN 978-981-18-7486-4

Gospel Partner™

GospelPartner.com

Printed in the Republic of Singapore

First edition

Contents

Introduction

Ever heard the phrase, "I worry because I care"?

And for those of us with many things that we care about—from the safety of our loved ones to the meals we have to put on the table, mortgages, our health, and so on—a lot of these cares can turn into an endless stream of worry that fills our minds at all times of the day.

Maybe on top of these daily worries, you've also been going through a seriously challenging season, and the added fears are more than you can handle. Maybe it's been your health or that of a loved one. Maybe it's being plunged into sudden debt. Maybe it's your spouse or a child you can't seem to connect with anymore. Or maybe you're slowly being eaten up by fears that you are no longer wanted, relevant, or enough in your family life, workplace, or society.

Whatever anxieties and fears you may be battling today—whether they're paralyzing fears or just worries you've come to accept as "normal"—I wrote this book for you.

You might be wondering: *Is it realistic to imagine we can live life without fear of the future when there's so much that needs our attention every single day? When we're living in such dark times?*

In response, the Bible tells us, "Can all your worries add a single moment to your life? . . . if God cares so wonderfully for wildflowers that are here today and thrown into the fire tomorrow, he will certainly care for you. Why do you have so little faith?" (Matt. 6:27, 30 NLT).

My friend, your worries and fears will begin to dissipate when you are reminded again and again that the One who loves you and cares most for you is also able to provide for you.

Today, whether you're worried about growing old, losing your job, or a bad health report, I want you to know these fears cannot continue to harass and torment you when you know and believe the perfect love of the Lord for you (1 John 4:18). And my prayer is that over the course of reading the 28 devotionals in this book, you will come to know and experience this unwavering, unconditional, and unfailing love of the Lord for you.

If the fear of not having enough in any area of life is troubling you, may you discover how our Lord Jesus is more than willing and able to supply every lack. He is your good Shepherd, lovingly watching over you, defending you from your enemies, settling your fears, leading you to safe places, and providing for every practical need.

If it's a health condition that has been giving you sleepless nights, may you discover how near He is to those who are afflicted, how He is your strength and your peace. But even more than this, may you experience your healing as you see how He went to the cross and suffered so that you can be delivered from your affliction—and not be tormented by thoughts that you won't.

And if you're anxious about your safety and that of your loved ones especially in these dangerous times, may you discover how the Lord is your all-round covering and protection. You don't have to be afraid of the arrow that flies by day, nor of the terror by night, nor of perilous pestilences that are increasingly part of life these days. Even when the adversity is great, you don't have to be afraid of the worst-case scenarios happening. Instead, may you find opportunities in each devotional you read to lean on His love, immerse yourself in His protection promises, and experience His deliverance.

Over the course of the 28 days, as you take time to meditate on the scriptures, on His words of grace, and on the uplifting personal testimonies you will find in this book, I pray you will tangibly experience the Lord Jesus' immeasurable and personal love for you. As you read each daily reading, ask Him to speak to you as you talk to Him honestly about your fears. I believe you will find the Lord encouraging you about your situation and imparting His hope and peace to you. As you use these readings to just spend time in His presence and draw from His unlimited love and supply, may you come away strengthened and full of peace, and see the Lord turn those areas of worry around for you.

I believe the Lord is just waiting to meet you at your point of need, my friend. Worrying is not going to change your situation, but discovering and standing on His love, His Word, and His promises for you certainly can!

Are you ready to take this journey together with me?

Let's get started!

01

"Peace I leave with you, My peace I give to you; not as the world gives do I give to you. ***Let not your heart be troubled, neither let it be afraid."***

John 14:27

Thought:

Let not your heart be troubled.

Are you feeling anxious or troubled about something right now? Maybe you find yourself caught in a difficult situation that seems impossible to resolve, and you can't stop worrying about it.

My friend, do you know Jesus is right there with you in the midst of those troubling thoughts, saying, "Peace be unto you!"?

You may be wondering how anyone can feel peaceful while surrounded by challenges. But when our Lord Jesus—the Prince of Peace Himself—steps into your situation, you can, because **He** imparts **His own peace**—His shalom—to you.

The Lord's *shalom* is a peace *not as the world gives*. It is not transient or easily shaken, but a deep-settled peace that says, "Don't worry, My child, I've got this." It's a peace that imparts harmony, wholeness, well-being, and preservation to you.

Today, whether it's some unsettling news you've heard or the weight of family responsibilities that is keeping you up at night, will you take up the Lord's invitation to "let not your heart be troubled"? Just tell Him, "Lord Jesus, I give You this worry, and I receive Your shalom-peace right now."

If I do that, does it mean my problems will just disappear?

No, they might not. But as our Lord said, "Can any one of you by worrying add a single hour to your life?" (Matt. 6:27 NIV).

Friend, we gain *nothing* by worrying. In fact, worrying only *steals* our peace and mental and emotional wellness. But when you choose to let Him into your situation, you're saying, "Lord, I'm entrusting my challenges into Your hands, and I refuse to let my rest be robbed."

As you rest in the Lord's love for you and simply receive His shalom-peace, you'll find His love and peace untangling your emotions and driving out every fear. And you'll find the Lord more than capable of looking after the areas of your life that are important to you.

02

But Jesus spoke to them at once. "Don't be afraid," he said. "Take courage. I am here!"

Matthew 14:27 NLT

Thought:

Keep your eyes on Jesus, not the storm.

When we are caught up in the storms of life, the sheer immensity of our challenges can make us feel like there is just no way out, and fear can hold our hearts in an icy grip.

In Matthew 14, we have an account of Jesus' disciples feeling this firsthand as they battled a violent storm on the Sea of Galilee. Then Jesus came walking on the water to them. And that's when Peter, at Jesus' command, stepped out onto the raging sea and walked on the water toward Him.

According to every law of science, there was no way Peter could have pulled off such a feat. But as long as his eyes were on the Lord, Peter remained above the waves and above the storm.

Beloved, this is how the Lord encourages us to overcome the difficulties we face in life. Not by looking at the magnitude and hopelessness of our situations and trying to overcome these odds on our own but by keeping our eyes on Jesus, the author and finisher of our faith (Heb. 12:2).

Maybe you're in the midst of a storm right now. It could be a devastating health challenge. Someone you love may have hurt you deeply or walked out on you. Or a job you were so hoping to land eluded you once more. Maybe you've been battling the waves of self-doubt and failure for the longest time. I know it's hard, but you don't have to give in to the darkness and despair that threaten to overwhelm you.

In your night season, see your loving Savior coming to you. Hear Him saying to you, "*Don't be afraid. Take courage. I am here.*" See Him in the midst of the storm, stilling every wind and boisterous wave for you.

And if we forget to keep our eyes on Him? I pray it encourages you to know that even when you become distracted and take your eyes off the Lord, **He never takes His eyes off you**—just as He never took His eyes off Peter. Jesus reached out to catch Peter in his moment of doubt as he started to sink.

As you keep your eyes fixed on Jesus and on His perfect love for you, know that as He is far above every storm of life, so are you in the face of any defeat, sickness, or trouble against you today (1 John 4:17). Take courage, my friend, the Lord is with you. He is your mighty Savior and very present help in times of trouble (Ps. 46:1)!

03

The God of my strength,
in whom I will trust;
my shield and the horn
of my salvation, my
stronghold and my refuge.

2 Samuel 22:3

Thought:

The Lord is your shield on every side.

My friend, if you are going through a dark season, God knows and understands the anxiety, fear, and frustration you feel. He knows it can be difficult to have hope and see the light when the night seems to be stretching on forever.

I'm so glad the Lord has given us a picture of His protection and security to reassure and strengthen us through dark and trying periods—the Lord Himself as our *shield*.

The Hebrew word for *shield* in 2 Samuel 22:3 is the word *magen*.[1] *Magen* comes from the root word *ganan*, meaning "to defend, to cover, to surround."[2]

Your heavenly Father is surrounding and covering you on all sides, even when you don't see or feel it. You don't have to be afraid because He will guard you against all attacks and threats—both the tangible ones and the invisible ones you battle in your mind!

Today, if you are battling dark and depressive thoughts or if you're feeling weak and vulnerable or overwhelmed, hear the Lord saying to you, "Do not be afraid. I AM your shield protecting you on all sides." When you can't fall asleep at night because of all the negative thoughts swirling in your mind, see yourself completely covered by Him—your mighty God who causes your enemies to melt like wax (Ps. 68:2).

With the Lord as your shield, you can rest securely even in your night season, knowing that no harm can or will come to you!

NOTES

1. OT: 4043, James Strong, *Biblesoft's New Exhaustive Strong's Numbers and Concordance of the Bible with Expanded Greek-Hebrew Dictionary*. Copyright © 1994, 2003, 2006 Biblesoft, Inc. and International Bible Translators, Inc.

2. OT: 1598, Joseph Henry Thayer, Francis Brown, Samuel Rolles Driver, and Charles Augustus Briggs, *The Online Bible Thayer's Greek Lexicon and Brown Driver & Briggs Hebrew Lexicon*. Copyright © 1993, Woodside Bible Fellowship, Ontario, Canada. Licensed from the Institute for Creation Research.

04

"Which of you by worrying can add one cubit to his stature? *If you then are not able to do the least, why are you anxious for the rest? . . . If then God so clothes the grass, which today is in the field and tomorrow is thrown into the oven, how much more will He clothe you."*

Luke 12:25–26, 28

Thought:

Let go and see God's supply flow.

Are there areas in your life that you find yourself unable to stop worrying about? Maybe it's a long-term health condition. Or your job. Or how to resolve a pressing problem in your marriage or parenting. Like fingers constantly picking at an itchy scab, maybe your thoughts keep circling back to these areas, robbing you of peace and rest.

Let me share with you something that will help break this habit and bring the Lord's supply into your negative situations.

Some years ago, the Lord gave me a vision of one of the main obstacles that stops us from receiving His supply. I saw soft golden pipes coming down from heaven toward a man, bringing a fresh and constant flow of God's supply to various areas of his life.

But the moment the man started worrying about a certain area, the pipe supplying that area became constricted. It was as though his worrying was a fist clenching the pipe.

Have you noticed that provision flows freely and easily in areas you are least worried about? Conversely, it is in the areas you are anxious about that supply is often lacking. The Lord's supply is constantly flowing in our lives, but our anxiety can hinder us from receiving it.

When God says, "Don't worry," He is saying to you, "Let go and let Me supply you." I want to encourage you to let go of that pipe, because God is already supplying what you need. As you let go and trust Him to come through for you in your situation, you'll receive the supply that is already freely flowing from Him!

05

It is vain for you to rise up early, to sit up late, to eat the bread of sorrows; for so ***He gives His beloved sleep.***

Psalm 127:2

Thought:

God gives His beloved sleep.

My friend, God wants you to sleep soundly and sleep well even during times of trouble. He longs to calm your heart and give "His beloved sleep."

The key to receiving this rest is one that we can learn from David, whose name means "beloved."[1] It takes a "David" to defeat a Goliath. It takes someone who knows he or she is beloved to knock down the enemy.

Today, the enemy may be trying to intimidate you with fear. He may be telling you, *You are never going to be healed* or *You're going to lose everything*. But when you know how much God loves *you*, fear won't stand a chance against you.

Friend, your heavenly Father loves you so much, He gave His only Son to pay the price for all your sins. Today, as His beloved child, you can enjoy intimacy with Him as well as the fullness of His forgiveness, health, protection, and power.

When you know you are deeply and unconditionally loved by your Father, you will have the unwavering assurance that He is on your side taking care of you. Your heavenly Father, who watches over you, neither slumbers nor sleeps (Ps. 121:3-4). And as you rest in His perfect love, you can lie down and go to sleep unafraid because you know He is tackling every problem troubling you and giving to you even as you sleep.

As you embrace the truth that you are a beloved son or daughter of God, may you begin to enjoy deep, restful sleep each night, knowing you are safe in His hands.

NOTE

1. OT: 1732, Joseph Henry Thayer, Francis Brown, Samuel Rolles Driver, and Charles Augustus Briggs, *The Online Bible Thayer's Greek Lexicon and Brown Driver & Briggs Hebrew Lexicon*. Copyright © 1993, Woodside Bible Fellowship, Ontario, Canada. Licensed from the Institute for Creation Research.

06

“Therefore do not worry, saying, ‘What shall we eat?’ or ‘What shall we drink?’ . . . For your heavenly Father knows that you need all these things. ***But seek first the kingdom of God and His righteousness, and all these things shall be added to you.*** *Therefore do not worry about tomorrow.”*

Matthew 6:31–34

Thought:

You don't have to worry about tomorrow.

Why is it so easy for us to get caught up in our worries?

Even as you're reading this right now, maybe your mind is occupied with all the ceaseless demands on you. Maybe you're mentally running through a list of things you need to handle, and there are people breathing down your neck. Maybe just thinking about what tomorrow will bring leaves you feeling helpless and defeated.

My friend, your heavenly Father knows all that you are responsible for and need to deal with. And His words of comfort to you are, "Do not worry about tomorrow."

This is His way of telling you, "Each day may have its own problems, but don't live tomorrow today. **There is**

grace for today, and when tomorrow comes, My grace will be there to meet you at your point of need."

Your loving Father already knows exactly what you need and when you need it. Isn't it a huge relief to know you don't need to meet all the demands of life yourself?

So will you take up the Lord's invitation to leave all your cares to your loving Abba Father?

I pray you'll take some time to meditate on and rest in His extravagant love and tender care for you. You'll find yourself enjoying His fresh supply for every challenge today and more than sufficient grace to take care of every need when tomorrow comes!

07

***Now to Him who is able to do exceedingly abundantly above all that we ask or think,** according to the power that works in us.*

Ephesians 3:20

Thought:

God's inexhaustible supply is always greater than your needs.

When you are faced with a lack, what do you choose to focus on? Our logical minds tell us to analyze the problem and use whatever resources we can scrape together to solve the problem.

The thing is, when you zoom in on the vastness of your need and the little you have in your hands, it can leave you feeling utterly overwhelmed.

In 2 Kings 4:1, we meet a widow who desperately sought the prophet Elisha's help to repay a large debt to the creditor. If she couldn't pay up, he was going to take her two children to be his slaves.

When Elisha asked her, "What do you have in the house?", she said, "Your maidservant has nothing in the house but a jar of oil" (2 Kings 4:2).

Imagine her surprise when that little jar of oil went on to fill and keep on filling the numerous vessels she had borrowed from her neighbors! In fact, it ceased only when she had run out of vessels.

The Lord's supply was limited only by the number of containers she had brought to the party. And His supernatural supply not only paid off her debt, but it also left her and her children with plenty to live on.

This is the same superabundant supply the Lord provides for you and your loved ones today. The Lord is not concerned about how much you have on hand because with Him even a little becomes **much** when you put it in His hands.

If you're battling worries today because you can't see how your little can meet the huge demand, may I encourage you to bring our Lord Jesus into your situation? He loves you and delights in not just meeting but over-supplying every area of lack!

08

*Your word is a **lamp to my feet** and a light to my path.*

Psalm 119:105

Thought:

Let God lead you one step at a time.

In the midst of a particularly dark season, life can feel so bleak and paralyzing you can barely get out of bed in the morning. If that's what you're going through today, I want to encourage you to take a deep breath, ask the Lord for His help, and take it one step at a time.

Live one day at a time. Get up, do what you are supposed to do, then do the next thing, and the next.

But what's the point of doing this when I don't even know where I'm headed?

My friend, even if you are not sure where the journey will take you, rest assured our Lord Jesus does. As you put your trust in Him, the Holy Spirit will lead you step by step to exactly where you need to go.

Psalm 119:105 tells us that God's Word is a "lamp to my feet." The Lord provides light for you to take **one step at a time**. Why? Because He wants you to live by His **daily manna** and not worry about what you need to do tomorrow.

It's like walking up a winding staircase. You may not be able to see where, or when, or how many more steps you'll have to take before it ends, but each step brings you closer to the top. In the same way, as you take one step at a time trusting the Lord, before you know it, He will lead you to a place of breakthrough.

Today, won't you trust the Lord and do what He leads you to do one small step at a time? Whether it's getting out of bed, going out for a walk, or just having one conversation, allow Him to lead you to the change and breakthrough you need.

09

And He said to me,
"My grace is sufficient
***for you**, for My strength is*
made perfect in weakness."
Therefore most gladly
I will rather boast in my
infirmities, that the power of
Christ may rest upon me.

2 Corinthians 12:9

Thought:

God's grace is attracted to your weakness.

Many of us have been conditioned to despise and be ashamed of our weaknesses and to only show our best selves whenever we are in front of others. We worry about our weaknesses because we're afraid they'll make people reject us.

But the Lord feels differently about our weaknesses. The Bible tells us He is **attracted** to our demerits because His miracle-working power is made perfect and complete in our weaknesses.

This is such a powerful truth! Where there is no weakness, His power and grace cannot flow and transform us.

Can you believe that? The Lord's grace is not **attracted** to your strength but to your weakness.

My friend, don't be ashamed of your weakness. Maybe it's a bad habit. Maybe it's terrible fear of something. Just come to the Lord with your weakness and say, "Lord, I thank You that because of my weakness, Your miracle-working power is flowing toward me right now."

When you begin to "boast" in your infirmities like this, just as Paul did, you'll start to experience the power of Christ resting upon you. You'll find His power supplying you the strength, wisdom, and favor you need even as He delivers you.

Whatever your weakness or inability today, you don't have to hide it from your loving Savior. You can come to Him just as you are, boldly receive His grace, and let it flow through your weakness so that His power manifests in you. May you freely receive His unmerited favor, strength, and help today and see Him move mightily in your life.

10

*And being in agony, He prayed more earnestly. Then **His sweat became like great drops of blood falling down to the ground.***

Luke 22:44

Thought:

The Lord's finished work has set you free from negative thoughts.

If you find yourself troubled by dark thoughts, I want you to know our Lord Jesus has borne this oppression on your behalf so that you can be set free from crippling fears, mounting anxiety, and deep hopelessness today. You see, He didn't just die for your sins but also paid for you to have victory over fear and negative thoughts.

In the middle of the night, hours before His betrayal and crucifixion, Luke 22:39-44 tells us that Jesus went to the garden of Gethsemane on the Mount of Olives to pray. During this time, He was in such agony at the thought of being separated from His Father and carrying the sins of the world that He began to sweat great drops of blood that fell to the ground.

This is a medical condition known as hematidrosis, where under extreme stress, the capillaries, especially around the brow, break. Sweat and blood mingle, causing the person to "sweat blood."

My friend, in those very moments of His agony in the garden, our Lord Jesus took your anguish, your anxieties, and every bit of your mental oppression upon Himself. His blood that cleanses and restores has redeemed and bought you out of your mental affliction.

But that's not all. Later Jesus also wore a crown of thorns (Matt. 27:29) that brutally pierced His head so that today, you can have a sound mind that's free from fear, depression, anxiety, and stress. He freed you from every curse and gave you His gift of righteousness so that you can be crowned with blessings (Prov. 10:6 NIV).

Each time you are troubled by dark, fearful, or stressful thoughts, remember that Jesus has borne all of your agony and fear and shed His blood so that you can walk in the full blessings of power, love, and a sound mind (2 Tim. 1:7).

11

*Love has been perfected among us in this: that we may have boldness in the day of judgment; because **as He is, so are we in this world.***

1 John 4:17

Thought:

As Jesus is, so are you in this world.

When you start comparing yourself with others, it can be easy to feel like you are not praying enough, not doing enough, and simply not good enough.

I want you to know that even though these thoughts seem like the truth, they are from the enemy. The devil will always point you to you—to your flaws and failures. But the Holy Spirit will always point you to **Jesus**.

In Exodus 28:36–38, the Bible tells us that as long as Israel's high priest was wearing the turban with the golden plate bearing the words, "HOLINESS TO THE LORD," the people were accepted by God.

Today Jesus is our great High Priest. He has paid the price for all our sins and failures, and because His thoughts are **always** pure and holy, we are accepted by God.

Even in our best efforts to honor the Lord in our thought life, we know our self-efforts will fail and fall short from time to time. The good news is that rather than judge us based on the perfection of our thoughts, He looks to Jesus and His thoughts! Today the question is not, "Am I good enough?" but "Is Jesus good enough?" And in Christ, you are as righteous and accepted by God as Jesus is (Eph. 1:6, 1 John 4:17).

My friend, if you're feeling like a failure or just feeling out of sorts in your physical health or emotions today, count on your perfect High Priest. See yourself in *Him*. Know that as Jesus is strong, healthy, and full of life, so are you in this world. And as Jesus is always victorious, so are you over the challenges in your life.

As you go about your day, see yourself overcoming your challenges and receiving God's overflowing blessings. Why? Because as Jesus is, so are you in this world!

12

And Jesus answered and said to her, "Martha, Martha, you are worried and troubled about many things. ***But one thing is needed, and Mary has chosen that good part****, which will not be taken away from her."*

Luke 10:41–42

Thought:

Only one thing is needed.

Have you been feeling frazzled, hassled, and stressed by all that you need to do with the little time you have? And maybe you feel that nobody understands the strain you are under as you take care of all the daily responsibilities.

If trying to manage all your responsibilities leaves you feeling dry, edgy, and flustered, I want you to know this: every day, one thing is needful, says the Lord, and that is to sit at His feet in a posture of receiving. He wants you to **sit down** (which can seem so hard when you're busy trying to make sure everything is taken care of) and receive His Word and His supply, just as Mary did (Luke 10:39).

Friend, our Lord Jesus is not like you and me. **He came specially to give, not to receive** (Matt. 20:28). He is so full of grace, and His heart is overflowing. It brings Him great joy to give to us!

And unlike us, no matter how much He gives, His supply is never depleted.

So don't allow yourself to be driven and distracted by the demands that are pressing on you, as Martha did (Luke 10:40). No matter how many things are calling for your attention, the best thing you can do for yourself and your family is to sit before the Lord and receive from Him all that you need.

As you rest and receive from Jesus daily, I pray that you will experience His inexhaustible supply, shalom-peace, practical wisdom, and right-place, right-time blessings flowing into every area of your life.

13

The Lord is my shepherd;
I shall not want. . . .
He leads me beside
the still waters.
He restores my soul.

Psalm 23:1–3

Thought:

Live in your Shepherd's love.

We know from the Scriptures that David was a powerful warrior and one of the greatest kings who ever lived. But what won him those victories and made him such a well-respected leader?

I believe it started back in his early years when he was a simple shepherd boy. From the words he wrote in Psalm 23—"The LORD is my shepherd"—David reveals the answer: he saw himself as a sheep and saw the Lord as his shepherd.

This precious secret empowered him to be comfortable being the person God had created him to be and to enjoy the fullness of life, despite having his fair share of trials and troubles. David knew how to live at rest because he lived in the love and care of his Shepherd.

With his Shepherd watching over him, he had no lack but plenty of supply. He didn't worry about his next destination but instead let his loving Shepherd lead him.

David knew to trust in and go to his Shepherd whenever his heart was troubled. And whenever he was attacked by his enemies, he knew how to look to the Lord for His protection, supply, and victory (Ps. 23:4-6).

Today, as you **see yourself as a sheep being watched over, led, and taken care of by your loving Shepherd**, you too can live life at rest and receive the blessings David did—even when you have to deal with less-than-ideal situations and people with unique needs. When you're being cared for by our Lord Jesus, the best shepherd, it'll give you the peace and confidence to shepherd others as well (as David did), be it in your family, workplace, or community.

Rest in your Good Shepherd's love and protection and know that you can live without stress and fear for He is watching over you and providing all that you need. He is looking after your future and leading you every step of the way.

14

But those who wait on the LORD shall renew their strength; they shall mount up with wings like eagles.

Isaiah 40:31

Thought:

God's hope strengthens you in your challenges.

Child of God, one thing that sets you apart from the world is that God has **promised** you hope in your times of trouble. To the world, hope is never certain—it's about holding out for something they are unsure will come to pass.

But for us believers, the Lord has given us **His** hope—a positive, confident expectation of good for our future (2 Cor. 1:7 AMP). You can expect a bright future where your needs are taken care of because your hope is anchored to something unshakable—the love of God poured out in our hearts by the Holy Spirit (Rom. 5:5).

Did you know that the Hebrew word for *hope* is *tiqvah*, which actually means "a cord"[1] or rope? *Tiqvah* comes from the verb *qavah*,[2] which means "to bind together" and is translated as the word *wait* in the well-known verse, "But those who wait [or hope] on the LORD shall renew their strength" (Isa. 40:31).

Today, if you're waiting for your breakthrough to manifest, the Lord wants you to stay in a posture of hope. And hope will remain strong in you as you see yourself tightly bound to the Lord, the way the strands of a rope are intertwined and bound together, giving it strength.

Whether the situation concerns your marriage, a bad medical report, or coming through a recession with no loss, know that you are not left alone to fend for yourself. As a believer, you are so utterly bound to and so completely one with our Lord Jesus that His peace, His protection, and His victory are yours.

Beloved, as you wait on the Lord like this and find your hope in Him, He will renew your strength, causing you to rise above your circumstances with Him. Despite your challenges, you will run and not be weary, you will walk and not faint (Isa. 40:31). Your hope in Him will not disappoint because He loves you, and He is working *all things* together for your good (Rom. 5:5, Rom. 8:28)!

NOTES

1. OT: 8615, James Strong, *Biblesoft's New Exhaustive Strong's Numbers and Concordance of the Bible with Expanded Greek-Hebrew Dictionary*. Copyright © 1994, 2003, 2006 Biblesoft, Inc. and International Bible Translators, Inc.

2. OT: 6960, James Strong, *Biblesoft's New Exhaustive Strong's Numbers and Concordance of the Bible with Expanded Greek-Hebrew Dictionary*. Copyright © 1994, 2003, 2006 Biblesoft, Inc. and International Bible Translators, Inc.

15

For you shall not go out with haste, nor go by flight; for ***the Lord will go before you,*** *and* ***the God of Israel will be your rear guard.***

Isaiah 52:12

Thought:

The Lord goes before you and guards you from behind.

When the children of Israel arrived at the Red Sea after leaving Egypt, they certainly weren't prepared to see Pharaoh's army furiously charging toward them, intent on either taking them back or taking them down. Hemmed in by an unyielding sea in front and by elite forces of a ruthless enemy from behind, all the Israelites could see was imminent death (Exod. 14:10–12).

Suddenly, the Angel of God, who had been leading the camp of Israel, moved behind them. The pillar of cloud that had been positioned in front of the camp also moved to the back and stood between the Israelites and the marauding Egyptian army.

This created a cloud of darkness for the Egyptians but provided light for the Israelites so that neither party came near the other throughout the night. And as the Israelites made their way through the parted Red Sea, Pharaoh's armies couldn't touch them. In fact, the Lord brought such confusion upon the enemy that even *they* could see the Lord was fighting for His people (Exod. 14:19-25)!

Beloved, whatever you're worried about—your child's grades, bills to pay, or protection for your family—**know that the Lord has already gone ahead of you to prepare the path before you take your next step**. Even if evil tries to strike you from behind, the Lord is your rear guard, protecting you from any harm before it reaches you.

And when you think you are out of options, remember the Lord who loves you is also the God of miracles. Just as He made a way for His people to pass through the waters of the Red Sea, He will bring confusion to the enemy and make a way for you. Fear not, child of God, for your God fights for you!

16

"Because he has sinned and is guilty . . . he shall restore its full value, add one-fifth more to it, and give it to whomever it belongs."

Leviticus 6:4–5

Thought:

Jesus restores 120 percent of all that you have lost.

Have you felt robbed in any way lately? Maybe someone lied about you, and it's robbed you of good standing with your colleagues or family members. Or maybe a poor financial decision or an addiction has caused your marriage to suffer or robbed you of hope of a good future. My friend, the Lord cares more about what has happened to you than you realize.

In the Old Testament, the law stated that if a person stole from another, he would need to make restitution as well as offer a trespass offering to the Lord. And to make restitution, the person guilty of wrongdoing would need to pay the full price of the loss suffered plus an additional

20 percent to the injured party. This meant the injured party ultimately became a gainer, receiving a 120 percent restoration for what he had lost.

My friend, do you know this blessing is yours in Christ?

You don't need to stay in resentment toward the person or situation that has robbed you. You don't have to be afraid of the future, seeing only further loss. You only need to turn your eyes to Jesus.

He became your trespass offering on the cross. He is not the one who stole from you, yet at the cross, He restored that which He took not away (Ps. 69:4 KJV). He made full restitution for you to have His much-more restoration for every wrong, every pain, and every loss you have suffered.

Today you can say to the Father, "Father, because Jesus became my trespass offering, I'm a candidate for 120 percent restoration. I receive it now for my finances/health/mind/marriage." And get ready to see His restoration make this area stronger than it was before!

17

"But I come to you in the name of the LORD of hosts, the God of the armies of Israel. . . . This day the LORD will deliver you into my hand. . . . Then all this assembly shall know that the LORD does not save with sword and spear; ***for the battle is the LORD's."***

1 Samuel 17:45–47

Thought:

The battle is the Lord's.

One of the greatest (and most unexpected) battles in the Bible is the one between David and Goliath. This battle was not famous for fighting prowess or glorious battle scenes. Instead, it was epic because a young shepherd boy defeated an intimidating, fully-armed, battle-seasoned giant with nothing more than a stone and sling. He wasn't even protected by armor!

David triumphed over Goliath because he knew something the giant didn't. He believed even before he faced Goliath that **the battle was the Lord's**. He knew that as he went to battle in the name of the Lord, God was the One who would deliver his enemy into his hands. Instead of putting his trust in himself and his own skills and abilities, David put His trust in the Lord.

Today your giant may be a bondage you've been battling for a long time. It could be an addiction, debt, a cycle of defeat, or a disease the doctors have said there is no cure for. Be like David and say to it, "The battle is the Lord's." Let go and see the Lord fight your battle. That's our greatest fight. That's the beautiful fight of faith.

You see, the Lord Jesus is stronger and greater than you are, and He is on your side (Rom. 8:31). He also knows your enemy better than you do. All He wants you to do is rest, depend on His strength, and let Him take over.

My friend, I'm believing with you that as you let go and let the Lord fight for you as David did, He'll give you a victory that's swifter and greater than anything you can imagine!

18

“These things I have spoken to you, that ***My joy may remain in you****, and that your joy may be full.”*

John 15:11

Thought:

Unshakable joy is yours.

During festive occasions in Israel, you'll hear Israelis saying, "*Chag sameach*!" to each other. *Chag* means "holiday," and *sameach* means "happy" or "joyful."[1] The Bible says that when you have a merry heart or a heart full of *sameach*, it does good to you, like medicine to a sick body.

My friend, the Lord wants you to be happy. Not just when things are going well for you but even when the going gets tough. On the night that Jesus was betrayed, He shared with His disciples His desire for His joy to remain in them and that their joy may be *full* (John 15:11). Just imagine that—knowing the horrors that awaited Him, He spoke to His friends about His *joy*. All the pain, sin, and sorrow He bore on the cross was so that we can *always* be full of joy through the complete forgiveness of our sins.

I know that when you're going through a difficult season, it's hard to feel joyful.

But this is why the Lord has given us His joy—so that after the negative feelings have rolled over us, we don't have to stay in despair, discouragement, or defeat. We can be joyful and even rejoice—because we know the grace of God is at work in our lives—and walk in healing and health. Anguish and sorrow, on the other hand, lead to a broken spirit, and oftentimes, sickness (Prov. 15:13, 17:22).

If you're feeling down today, can I encourage you to spend time in the Lord's reassuring presence and just talk to Him about it? I believe hope and joy will arise in your heart as He reminds you that He loves you, He's got it covered, and His grace is working all things out for your good (Rom. 8:28).

NOTE

1. "Chag Sameach," *The Jewish Chronicle*, accessed November 25, 2022, https://www.thejc.com/judaism/jewish-words/chag-sameach-1.5928.

19

He will cover you with
his feathers. He will
shelter you with his wings.

Psalm 91:4 NLT

Thought:

You are safe under His wings of protection.

With natural disasters, unrest, and health crises dominating the news today, it can be hard not to feel uneasy about your family's or your own safety.

Child of God, your heavenly Father doesn't want you living in constant fear that bad things will happen to you. Rather, He wants you to live bold and free, knowing that you are covered by His protection.

The enemy may try to instill fear by telling you that you might be next, but these thoughts need not dominate and intimidate you. Just as a mother hen protectively gathers her chicks under her wings, the Lord wants to shield you under His wings and protect and deliver you from the enemy's snares and attacks (Ps. 91:3, Matt. 23:37).

But how can we live confident of the Lord's protection and walk in wisdom in these days? God's Word gives us a key in Jude 1:21 NLT, which tells us to **keep ourselves safe in the love of God**. The Greek word for "keep" is *tereo*, which means "to guard from loss or injury."[1]

In other words, the more you are conscious of the Father's love enveloping you throughout the day, the more you will see how close you are to God's heart and experience protection under His wings. And in this secret place of the Most High, you'll also find the Lord leading you with His wisdom and putting you at the right place at the right time.

My friend, our Lord Jesus, the mighty One who shelters you under His wings, says to you today, "**Do not be afraid** of the terrors of the night, nor the arrow that flies in the day. **Do not dread** the disease that stalks in darkness, nor the disaster that strikes at midday" (Ps. 91:5-6 NLT). You can go about each day confident that the Lord's protection guards you and your loved ones.

NOTE

1. NT: 5083, James Strong, *Biblesoft's New Exhaustive Strong's Numbers and Concordance of the Bible with Expanded Greek-Hebrew Dictionary*. Copyright © 1994, 2003, 2006 Biblesoft, Inc. and International Bible Translators, Inc.

20

Then the children of Israel groaned because of the bondage . . . and their cry came up to God . . . and God acknowledged them.

Exodus 2:23-25

Thought:

Just a groan will reach the Father’s throne.

Do you know that you don’t need to pray long prayers for God to answer you? One of the most heartfelt and powerful prayers in the Bible was the one uttered by the children of Israel after years of harsh slavery in Egypt. So what did their prayer sound like?

It was simply a **groan**, a cry from the depths of their hearts!

And why do I say it was powerful?

Because the Lord not only heard it, but He also moved swiftly and sent them a deliverer.

What’s in a groan? Nothing fancy or eloquent, just a wordless sigh of wretchedness from deep inside in response to, well, wretched circumstances.

But see what happens when you groan to the Lord: Exodus 6:5–8 tells us that when the Lord heard His people groan, He remembered His covenant with them and declared that He would:

- Rescue and deliver them from bondage.
- Redeem them with His outstretched arm.
- Take them as His people and be their God.
- Bring them into their promised land.
- Give them the land as a heritage.

Wow! Talk about over-answering their needs—just because of a groan.

Am I saying we don't need to pray or talk to the Lord anymore? Of course not. Your Father in heaven loves to spend time with and hear from you. But in those moments you feel all prayed out, when you feel so battered by fear and anxiety, and all you can manage is a sigh or a groan, know it's more than enough for the Lord.

Just a groan will reach His throne.

If you can't find the words to pray today, find comfort in knowing that you can just cry out to your Abba Father, who, upon hearing even your softest sigh, will come swiftly to you and deliver you from your troubles.

21

Casting all your care upon Him, for ***He cares for you.***

1 Peter 5:7

Thought:

Jesus is the friend you can confide in.

When you need to rant or pour out your feelings, who do you turn to?

There is a Friend who loves and cares for you deeply, never condemns you, and is a shoulder for you to lean on always. His name is Jesus, and you can tell Him anything!

Too often, we are caught up with the idea that we can only talk to the Lord when we set aside undivided time and a specific place to pray. But He loves nothing more than for you to simply pour out your heart to Him wherever you are. That's also a form of prayer.

When you are driving, doing housework, or taking a walk, you can tell Him candidly, "Lord, this is troubling me right now," and share your worries with Him just as you would your closest friend.

I've discovered that the more open we are when we talk to Jesus, the closer we draw to Him and the more able we are to receive from Him. After talking to Him about what's on your heart, before you can even ask, "Lord, give me the grace for . . . ," you'll find He has already imparted strength to you. By the end of your heart-to-heart talks with Jesus, you can't help but sense that something has changed and, somehow, you aren't so anxious and discouraged anymore.

What's troubling you today? Is it a relationship that seems to be getting worse? Money worries? A series of failures that has mired you in self-doubt and anxiety?

You can be real and honest with your greatest Friend, Jesus. He loves you with a personal love and cares about every detail of your life. He is always by your side to comfort and strengthen you and to walk with you through all your challenges.

22

*"Now the blood shall be
a sign for you on the houses
where you are. And **when
I see the blood, I will pass
over you**; and the plague
shall not be on you
to destroy you."*

Exodus 12:13

Thought:

The blood of Jesus speaks forgiveness, protection, and blessings over you.

In one of the darkest nights known to the children of Israel—the night of their very first Passover—the Lord gave them hope and protection in the form of the blood of lambs.

The Lord had told His people that at midnight, the destroyer would be released upon the land as punishment on the Egyptians. The Israelites were to apply the blood of sacrificial lambs on their doorposts and lintels and prepare to leave Egypt. The Lord promised them that when He saw the blood, He would not permit the destroyer to enter their houses.

Were the Israelite families behind those doors perfect, guiltless people? No. But because the blood meant that an innocent life had been taken in their place, the plague had no right to destroy them.

Today the enemy may whisper to you, *You haven't done anything right this week. You don't deserve God's protection. You can't expect healing or that situation to turn around.* Whatever the area you're worried about, that's how he often gets you afraid and unable to rest.

How do you deal with his accusations and the doubts he plants in your mind?

My friend, just stand unafraid for you know that the divine, sinless blood of Jesus, **the** Lamb of God, has been shed for you. His blood has cleansed you of all your sins and failures and made you righteous in God's sight. Today you have a blood-bought right to receive His protection, provision, healing, as well as godly wisdom to conduct all your affairs successfully.

Today, because God sees the blood of the innocent Lamb shed for your complete forgiveness, He will not allow any judgment, disease, or curse to harm you. You can rest secure in the power of Jesus' blood covering, delivering, and saving you and your household.

23

*"Only do not rebel against the Lord, nor fear the people of the land, for **they are our bread**; their protection has departed from them, and the Lord is with us. Do not fear them."*

Numbers 14:9

Thought:

See your problems as bread for you.

How do you see the problems that come your way? Do you see them as something that depletes you? Or do you see your challenges as bread, something the Lord can use to strengthen you?

At Kadesh Barnea, when Joshua and Caleb were sent together with ten others to spy out the promised land, the other spies returned with a negative report, saying there was little chance for them against the great walls and physically stronger Canaanites. They saw themselves as grasshoppers and believed the giant Canaanites would eat them for lunch (Num. 13:31-33)!

However, Joshua and Caleb had a different report. They said their enemies were "bread" for them. In other words, **they** would consume their enemies.

How could these two guys be so sure? Because they knew and believed this: **the Lord is with us** (Num. 14:9). That was how they could see the giants as something to make them stronger.

And because they knew this, they were not intimidated by how huge the enemies or their walls were. Joshua and Caleb were confident that since the Lord, the One who opened up the Red Sea, was on their side, He would defeat the giants and bring the Israelites into the land.

What are you worried about, my friend? Is the specter of failure or the enormity of your lack making you feel vulnerable and stealing your peace? Have recent setbacks made you feel insignificant and hopeless?

As the Lord Jesus was with His people and for them at Kadesh Barnea, so He is **with** you and **for** you (Heb. 13:5, Rom. 8:31). He delights in you and will conquer your giants for you. He will make them bread for you. See yourself emerging stronger as you rest in Him and let Him fight for you.

24

God is our refuge and strength, a very present help in trouble.

Psalm 46:1

Thought:

Jesus is your very present help in trouble.

My friend, do you find yourself caught up in regret over something negative that has happened to you? Or anxious about things that could go wrong tomorrow?

The first is living in the past. The second is living in the future. And both are going to rob you of peace and enjoyment of life in the **present**.

The Lord wants us to live in the present, enjoying His grace that is more than sufficient for today's needs. This is why faith deals with the present, the now. Hebrews 11:1 says, "**Now** faith **is** the substance of things hoped for, the evidence of things not seen." Notice how **faith** is sandwiched between the words **now** and **is**—both of which apply to the present.

Beloved, your loving Savior doesn't want you to live worried about the future or bound by hurts from the past and unable to see what He is doing in your life *in the present moment*. The Bible says our Lord Jesus is "a very **present** help in trouble" (Ps. 46:1) and that "*now* is the day of salvation" (2 Cor. 6:2). In other words, the Lord wants you to see and believe that His peace, wisdom, provision, and all of His saving power is available to you and working on your behalf *right now*.

Are you blaming yourself for something that happened in the past? Or worried that you won't be able to deal with a difficult situation tomorrow? Believe the Lord is your **present** help, and you won't have to live life trapped in the past or in fear of the future. You'll find Him in the midst of your challenges, supplying your needs, leading you, and protecting you from harm.

Rest in the Lord's love for you, my friend, and receive His grace and supply moment by moment. You'll find life infinitely less stressful and much more enjoyable!

25

But let us who are of the day be sober, putting on . . . as a helmet the hope of salvation.

1 Thessalonians 5:8

Thought:

Put on the helmet of salvation against the enemy's attacks.

One of the hardest things we face when going through difficult times is dealing with the slew of dark thoughts. They could come as feelings of hopelessness, maybe even blasphemous thoughts against God, or mind games that convince you to give up on life.

These thoughts may seem real and compelling, but they are actually from the enemy. He is constantly seeking to attack your mind, and one of his key tactics is to use the personal pronoun in the thoughts he puts in your mind. Thoughts such as, ***I** am such a failure* or *God has forsaken **me***.

You and I need to understand that even though dark thoughts enter our mind, we do not have to let them control us. We can put on as a helmet, the hope of salvation that we have in Christ to protect our minds from the devil's assaults.

You see, the word "salvation"—*soteria*—doesn't just mean saved from hell, but also saved from sickness, lack, and dangers in everyday life.[1] So to put on the hope of salvation as a helmet is to have a confident expectation that your loving Savior will heal you, provide for you, and save you out of every trouble.

When defeatist thoughts try to bring you to despair, guard your mind with this truth: *My hope in seeing God's saving power has a rock-solid foundation! Because Jesus paid for my sins on the cross, I have the forgiveness of sins, healing, and deliverance from every curse. God is FOR me, and I have a good future!*

Today won't you put on the hope of salvation as a helmet to guard your mind against all insidious thoughts from the enemy? I'm praying that as you do, you'll walk in the peace, soundness of mind, and protection for all areas of life that the Lord has freely given you!

NOTE

1. NT: 4991, William Edwy Vine, *Vine's Expository Dictionary of Biblical Words*. Copyright © 1985, Thomas Nelson Publishers.

26

The entrance of
Your words gives light;
it gives understanding
to the simple.

Psalm 119:130

Thought:

The Word of God brings light and life to your situation.

As you navigate uncertain or even difficult paths in life, know that God has already provided the answers you need for each step of the journey. He has given you a lamp that will light your way—the Word of God.

Psalm 119:130 says that God's Word gives light that even the simple can understand. When you are feeling confused and at a loss as to what to do, His Word will help you to see what you need to do, much like how turning on a light in a dark room helps you to locate a missing item.

The psalmist says it like this: "In Your light we see light" (Ps. 36:9). The insight, direction, and peace you seek is found in the Bible!

Maybe you're reading this and thinking, *I hear you, Pastor Prince, but I'm honestly so discouraged with what I've been going through that I can't find the desire to read the Bible.*

My friend, don't see reading the Bible as an extra burden. Instead, come to the Word seeing the Lord waiting to love you, comfort you, guide you, and strengthen you.

When you open your Bible, ask the Holy Spirit to show you the Lord Jesus and His grace. He may lead you to read the gospels, where just reading the accounts of our Lord compassionately supplying and healing all who came to Him will bring a cleansing, healing, and life-giving effect to your body, your mind, and to every dark situation (Prov. 4:22).

Whether you are facing financial lack, broken relationships, sickness, or struggling with self-doubt and depression, I want to encourage you to open up God's Word and let it breathe life, wisdom, and power into your situation. You can start with a single verse or a bite-size devotional each day. As you chew on His Word and let it refresh and infuse hope into your heart, you will see God's help and provision spring forth in your areas of lack!

27

And hope does not put us to shame.

Romans 5:5 ESV

Thought:

Unfailing hope is yours.

Have you ever found yourself managing your own expectations and not daring to believe for too much because you're afraid you'll be disappointed?

My friend, our God is a **God of hope** (Rom. 15:13), and He wants us to know that when we put our hope in Him and His love for us, this hope will not fail us. It will not put us to shame.

Unlike the hope the world has, Bible hope is a **confident expectation of good**. Instead of uncertainty, doubt, and anxiety, you are filled with a positive and joyful expectation of favorable things happening for you, of good happening in your future. And this is how the Father wants you, His beloved child, to live every day.

Do you find yourself more worried about your health as you advance in age? Instead of seeing yourself getting weaker, the Lord wants you to confidently expect that He, the nourisher of your old age, is daily restoring and adding health and strength to you (Ruth 4:15).

Maybe you're struggling with an addiction. My friend, don't see yourself permanently trapped in it. See the Lord's superabounding grace invading this area of weakness and expect to emerge freer and stronger than you've ever been (Rom. 5:20).

But Pastor Prince, can God be so good to a person like me?

Beloved, the reason you can expect good from God is that at the cross, Jesus bore the full punishment for all your sins and failures so that you can be blessed with every blessing (Eph. 1:3). God is not holding your sins against you, and He only has good plans for your future (Jer. 29:11 NLT).

Today, because of the cross, you can live free from fear and hopelessness. Instead of seeing things going from bad to worse, see yourself healthy, strong, and victorious in every area of life. Raise your hopes high and have an audacious and confident expectation that these positive, faith-filled visions will come to pass!

28

"And be sure of this:
***I am with you always**, even*
to the end of the age."

Matthew 28:20 NLT

Thought:

The Lord has promised never to leave nor forsake you.

When you love someone, you want to be close to them and even take on their burdens if you could. If you've ever cared for a sick child or an ailing loved one, I'm sure there were times you wished you could not just comfort them but also carry their pain in your own body so that they wouldn't have to suffer.

If we as imperfect human beings can feel this way, how much more our Lord Jesus, who loves us with a perfect love? When our hearts are full of worry or when trouble comes, He wants us to know He is so close to us, and He wants us to let Him carry those cares (1 Pet. 5:7 AMP).

While we are powerless to carry the pain of our loved ones, our Lord, in His great love for us, became our perfect substitute and carried our pains and sufferings on the cross (Isa. 53:4–5). In those long hours on that cross, He bore our sins as well as our diseases and pains. He went through mental torment in our place so that today, we can live free from everything that robs us of an abundant life.

Is your heart broken because of the words or actions of a loved one? Maybe you're recovering from an illness or trauma. My friend, our Lord Jesus is no stranger to our pain and suffering. He is our great High Priest who understands our weaknesses, and He invites you to come boldly to His throne of grace to receive whatever supply you need (Heb. 4:14–16 NLT).

As you go about your day, remember you have a loving Savior who not only empathizes with your sorrows but has also redeemed you from them. Whatever you're going through, you can tell Him all your worries and cares, knowing He understands and will move on your behalf to heal, protect, and provide for you.

Beloved, may you live confidently and fear-free as you rest more and more in the One who loves you and who will never leave you nor forsake you. Amen!

Closing Words

Dear friend, I pray that you have been encouraged by the thoughts in this book and have found the Lord imparting peace and hope in your areas of worry and fear.

And in taking this 28-day journey with me, I pray you've come away warmed by His love for you and eager to take the personal and intimate relationship He wants to have with you to the next level. You see, letting go of our worries and fears to the Lord is a daily, moment-by-moment decision, and it becomes easier as you keep practicing His love and His presence day by day.

Every day, live conscious that your loving Father in heaven is always with you, loving you, and caring about the things you are fearful or anxious about. The more you cultivate a strong sense of His perfect His love for you, the more you'll be quick to cast every care to Him and find rest in His sure promises for you.

Shall we do that now? Would you give me this opportunity to pray a blessing over you? I believe the Lord is more than ready to impart His shalom-peace to your heart and mind and to every troubling circumstance in your life right now. Let's pray:

Father, I thank You that in You, each and every one of Your precious children has a blessed future and true hope—a positive expectation of good that has been paid for with the finished work of Your Son, Jesus, on the cross.

Father, for those who are facing fear, worry, or anxiety right now, I speak Your shalom-peace that surpasses all understanding over them. As they rest in You, may they know that You are protecting them from every harm, fighting their battles for them, and moving behind the scenes to make all things work together for their good.

No matter how challenging the journey, I know You are right beside them, strengthening and lifting them up in Your hand. And I know that You will bring wholeness, supply, and restoration to their hearts, relationships, health, careers, finances, and any other areas that might be keeping them up at night.

Thank You, Father, that with this assurance, they need not have a troubled heart but can come boldly to Your throne of grace to receive mercy and grace to help them in their time of need. Thank You that they can look forward to breakthroughs, blessings, and restoration in the days to come. In Jesus' name, amen!

My friend, as you receive this prayer today, may you live carefree and with shalom-peace because you know that your heavenly Father Himself is supplying every need and meeting every care in your life!

I sincerely pray that you have been greatly blessed by this resource. Before you go, I have personally shortlisted several letters and praise reports from people who have been liberated from fear. I believe that their testimonies and breakthroughs will strengthen your heart to believe the Lord for your own breakthrough and not give up! I look forward to reading your testimony one day.

With love,

Praise Reports

Finally Free from Oppressive Thoughts

A few years into my marriage, I came under an intense attack. Fear, anxiety, and thoughts of death followed me around day and night. I would cry and shut myself away from everyone. It was so debilitating at times.

All I could do was pray in the Spirit and resist those thoughts and feelings that I knew were not from God. These thoughts would creep in daily to bring fear, and sometimes I would suddenly wake up from my sleep with startling thoughts and fears.

After six years of crying out to God for answers, I came across Joseph Prince's teachings, and as I learned about the gospel of grace, tears streamed down my face.
I always knew my Savior loved me, but I never knew the price He paid for me. I never knew all my sins, ugliness,

and guilt were laid on Him at the cross. I never knew His finished work was perfect or that I'm completely forgiven—past, present, and future.

I began to dig deeper into Pastor Prince's teachings by listening to sermons online, watching his television broadcasts, listening to podcasts, and reading all his books. Little by little over six years, I began to experience freedom. The nagging fears and anxieties left, and I began to see myself loved, protected, and provided for in every area of my life.

I began to see my children as loved and protected under the wings of our loving Father. My husband also began to hunger for the truth of God's Word and joined me in reading Joseph's books and watching his sermons. He now wakes up early to spend time with the Lord. We have witnessed miracles in our company and our marriage has also deepened into a stronger and sweeter one.

We are not perfect, but we have learned that even in the moments we are weak, God's love doesn't waver. He still sees us in Christ, and as He is, so are we in this world. We now live life unafraid as we rest in His unfailing grace and love.

We are not perfect, but we have learned that even in the moments we are weak, God's love doesn't waver. He still sees us in Christ, and as He is, so are we in this world. Whenever I feel stressed or anxious, I will say under my breath, "I am the righteousness of God in Christ, my loving Savior!" We now live life unafraid as we rest in His unfailing grace and love.

Thank you, Pastor Prince, for your boldness in following the Lord as He has given you this revelation of His Word. Your ministry and family are always in our prayers.

Winnie | Georgia, United States

Rested in Jesus and Scored Well in Exam

I am a first-year medical student in the United Kingdom. God gave me the desire to become a doctor, but I experienced difficulties keeping up with the demands of the course and would easily get stressed and drained. I felt discouraged as I'd always been an excellent student in secondary school.

My boyfriend introduced me to Joseph Prince a while back, but I didn't apply his teachings on grace until I had to prepare for an examination. When the exam was nearing, I felt ill prepared and suffered panic attacks due to intense worrying.

It was then that I decided to turn to Joseph Prince's teachings and watch his sermon entitled *Rest in Jesus' Faith for Miracles*. The sermon really touched me as I always felt weak in my faith and would feel condemned and not know how to stop the condemnation.

The sermon taught me to rest in Jesus' faith and not

mine—my faith is weak while His is unshakable. I knelt down at the end of the sermon and with faith that I never had before, asked Him to grant me a score of 71 percent for the upcoming exam.

On the day of the exam, I felt strangely calm. It was supernatural because I always felt incredibly nervous during exams. When the results were out, I got higher than what I had prayed for.

I felt an assurance of the victory that I already had in Christ, which spurred me on to study. And whenever worry and anxiety started to creep in, I would rest in His faith and confess that I am more than a conqueror through Him.

On the day of the exam, I felt strangely calm. It was supernatural because I always felt incredibly nervous during exams. Thank You, Jesus, for clearing my mind of stress and worry!

I went into the exam hall feeling victorious and came out feeling the same way. My peers said the exam was tough, but I thought it was fine. When the results were out, I got higher than what I had prayed for—
a score of 74 percent!

Thank you, Pastor Prince, for allowing God to teach His ways of grace through you.

Orlina | United Kingdom

No Longer Burdened by Worries and Anxieties

I was blessed to have stumbled upon Joseph Prince's program on a Christian broadcasting network three years ago. Every time I tuned in, I could feel the divine presence of the Lord.

I had been struggling with depression and anxiety caused by the demands of raising my children as a single, working mother. I was blessed to have their father in their lives, but it was still lonely and difficult at times.

When I watched Pastor Prince's broadcast, the downward spiraling of depression and the oppression I was under became less and less. I would cry healing tears and could feel emotional and spiritual healing taking place in

I started to go to Jesus more in prayer, trusting Him for peace, provision, supernatural favor, and daily guidance. I focused on worshiping Him and spending more time in His presence—being a Mary rather than a Martha.

me supernaturally because of the strong presence of the Lord Jesus.

When I watched Pastor Prince's *Live the Let-Go Life* sermon series, I began to let go of worries, anxieties, health issues, and fears of the future. I started to go to Jesus more in prayer, trusting Him for peace, provision, supernatural favor, and daily guidance. I focused on worshiping Him and spending more time in His presence—being a Mary rather than a Martha.

Since then, I have been richly rewarded spiritually and find myself sharing about Jesus' peace and guidance with other anxious, stressed-out people.

A sincere, heart-felt "thank you," Pastor Prince, for all your teachings. Your heart for the Lord and His Word has blessed so many.

To God be the glory!

Cindy | Florida, United States

Freed from Anxiety and Porn Addiction

Pastor Prince, I would like to thank you for sharing the gospel of grace without compromise. I've experienced many great victories since listening to your preaching. I'm thankful that my parents would play your television program when I was younger because when I went through a tough time a few years ago, I remembered you and started watching your videos on YouTube.

This was during a time in college when I was struggling with anxiety and sleeplessness. I also questioned my salvation. It was a fear that never really went away since accepting Jesus as my Savior when I was a child.

I'm reminded every day of my eternal salvation whenever I partake of the Lord's Supper and celebrate how I am washed completely clean by the blood of Jesus.

As I listened to your sermons and read your books, I started to experience amazing peace. I am now confident that my salvation can never be taken away from me! I'm reminded every day of my eternal salvation whenever I partake of the Lord's Supper and celebrate how I am washed completely clean by the blood of Jesus. I've also stopped watching porn effortlessly, a habit that used to make me feel so dirty and guilty.

Through your teachings on living the let-go life and praying in the Spirit, anxiety doesn't have a hold on me anymore! I'm excited to see more changes in my life as I grow in the knowledge of my Lord and Savior, Jesus Christ.

Joash | Ohio, United States

No More Tormented by Fears over Son

I used to be very fearful about my son's well-being. I would imagine him falling, getting hurt, or dropping dead in every possible scenario, and it nearly drove me crazy! These thoughts and imaginations really tortured me. They grew worse as he grew older because he's an active boy and my only child. I was known as "monster mama" in his school because I complained a lot about their safety standards.

Nobody was able to help me. All they told me was that I worry too much and suggested I let go and let my child grow up naturally. I wanted to stop all those thoughts but I just could not help myself! I had to shut down my social media account because I could not stand to read any more bad news. Doing that helped me a little, but the fearful thoughts continued in my head.

One day I heard Pastor Prince teach on meditation. He said that when he was afraid or scared, he would recite the Word of God over and over until that fear went away because the Word of God is alive and powerful. I tried to recite the verse that he used from 2 Timothy 1:7, but it did not yield any results for me. I felt discouraged until I stumbled upon this Romans 6:9 verse: "Death no longer has dominion over Him."

One day, I suddenly became aware that my fear was no longer as strong as before. It's because of Jesus that I can be normal and not be tormented by negative thoughts regarding my son's safety!

I know "Him" refers to Jesus, but because I have been listening to "as Jesus is so am I in this world," I changed the verse to, "Death no longer has dominion over me." I would quote this verse whenever the fears came: "Death no longer has dominion over me and my son." I just muttered it all day long even when I did not understand it completely.

I lost track of how long I was quoting Romans 6:9. But one day, I suddenly became aware that my fear was no longer as strong as before. It had loosened its grip over my mind. I could relax when it came to my son. Now I don't think about his safety in school 24/7 anymore.

Sometimes I still imagine bad things happening, but now it's like five on a scale of one hundred. Not only that, the Holy Spirit opened up Romans 6:9 for me. I realized that it is not just about death but also sicknesses, diseases, calamities, accidents, stress, aging, and so on. All things fallen in this world no longer have dominion over me! No wonder the Holy Spirit picked this particular verse for me. It applied to me perfectly!

My friends say I worry less now because my son is older. Ha! That's certainly not the reason. It's because of Jesus that I can be normal and not be tormented by negative thoughts regarding my son's safety!

I want to encourage everyone who is facing a similar problem: The world may not understand you and what you are going through. They may even label you as ridiculous, crazy, or a maniac, but God understands you, and He is more than willing to help you!

Thank you, Pastor Prince, for preaching the true gospel. Thank You, Lord Jesus!

Ina | South East Asia

Freed from Fears After Meditating on God's Word

For two years, I feared so much for my life that I couldn't drive or sleep with the doors unlocked.

Moreover, I misinterpreted Joshua 1:8 and thought I had to meditate on Scripture all the time to *earn* God's blessings. As a result, I felt discouraged from Bible meditation and believed this was the reason for my failures.

When Pastor Prince taught that Bible meditation is simply muttering God's Word under our breath as we go about each day, I felt relieved. Now I enjoy meditating on Scripture and have seen success in many areas—my one-year-old business is thriving in a tough economy, and I'm building my dream home debt-free.

Not only that, I can now drive without fear. Whenever I feel anxious, I would mutter the Word of God and feel better. I've also been encouraged by Pastor Prince's teachings on God's protection in Psalm 91. I would read and confess the psalm before going to bed. Unlike before, I can now fall asleep unafraid, even with my bedroom door wide open.

I can now drive without fear. Whenever I feel anxious, I would mutter the Word of God and feel better. I've also been encouraged by Pastor Prince's teachings on God's protection in Psalm 91. I would read and confess the psalm before going to bed. Unlike before, I can now fall asleep unafraid, even with my bedroom door wide open.

I'm truly grateful for Pastor Prince's ministry. I listen to his messages daily on the Joseph Prince app and have learned how to rightly interpret Scripture and enjoy reading the Bible. I've also been freed from self-condemnation after hearing about my righteousness in Christ. Hallelujah!

May God continue to bless Pastor Prince's ministry and free more souls for Jesus. Shalom!

Annika | South Africa

Delivered from Deep Depression

A number of years ago, I lost my house and vehicle after being cheated in business. I went into a deep depression and lost about 12 kg. I pulled myself out of every social gathering, which worsened my condition.

In my days of deep depression, I watched Pastor Prince's television program *Destined to Reign*, and he was sharing on how there is no more condemnation for those who are in Christ. This really lifted me up, and I was in awe of his message about God's grace. Growing up, I was never taught about this loving and gracious Jesus. I began listening regularly to Pastor Prince's sermons and learned that as my heavenly Father's child, He would protect me and provide for my every need.

One day, I surrendered my situation to Jesus and said, "This is not my battle. From now on, this is Your battle." I was referencing the verse in Exodus 14:14—"The Lord will fight for you, and you shall hold your peace."

From then on, the terror I felt disappeared drastically, and I began to enjoy life. I became addicted to listening to Pastor Prince's sermons, and the Bible became very interesting to me and my family. I needed to listen to at least one sermon a day to keep me reminded of the magnificent Father God I have. Every time I heard a powerful Word, I'd share it with my friends on social media and many of them also happily received the *metanoia* word for themselves.

The Lord did so many more good works in my life. I've gained back the weight I'd lost and made a lot of new friends. The Lord also lifted up my business and finances and took care of my family relationships during the hard times. My Abba also opened the way for me to get a new house and vehicle. Jesus' finished work on the cross has restored everything I'd once lost!

> *One day, I surrendered my situation to Jesus and said, "This is not my battle. From now on, this is Your battle." From then on, the terror I felt disappeared drastically, and I began to enjoy life. Jesus' finished work on the cross has restored everything I'd once lost!*

Thank you, Pastor Prince, for always teaching on the Lord's abundant grace.

Jack | South East Asia

Set Free from Drug Addiction, Experiencing Restoration

About four years ago, I was addicted to drugs and lost everything—my home, my job, my family, and my self-respect. One night, I was wandering the streets, high and homeless, when the weight of everything came crashing down on me. I collapsed to my knees and wept uncontrollably for some time, crying out, "God, I'm so messed up, and I don't know what to do. Help me!"

All of a sudden, I felt as if God had just reached into my brain and plucked out the addiction. I got up and noticed the urge was gone, like it was never there in the first place. This all happened without any withdrawal symptoms, and I haven't had the desire to indulge since.

It hasn't always been easy, but with the support I have and through constant listening to Pastor Prince's sermons and spending time In the Word, the Lord has taken me from glory to glory. My mind is being renewed, and life is getting better.

Since then, things have consistently gotten better. I have a job and vehicle now, my son is living with me again, and I get lots of time with my four-and-a-half-year-old daughter. God has also led me to a fantastic family in a faith-based church very near to the home He provided me. Through this amazing church family, I started doing outreach in the most impoverished community riddled with addiction and homelessness.

It hasn't always been easy, but with the support I have and through constant listening to Pastor Prince's sermons and spending time in the Word, the Lord has taken me from glory to glory. My mind is being renewed, and life is getting better. Praise God for answering my prayer and for His divine intervention.

I want to say a huge "thank you" to you, Pastor Prince. Your messages on God's grace, healing, and rest have been of more help than I can put into words. Whenever I drive, I'm almost always listening to one of your messages and praying in the Spirit.

All glory goes to the Lord for everything good in my life. I would not be where I am today without His grace, mercy, and guidance.

Jerry | Canada

Health and Mental Well-Being Restored

A few years ago, I experienced my first series of anxiety and panic attacks.

For six months, I experienced fear, anxiety, panic attacks, insomnia, and nightmares. I was not able to function during the day without help and couldn't play with my kids because of fatigue, chest pains, migraines, and all sorts of other symptoms. I cried out to God saying, "Lord! What is this? Where are You? Are You seeing what's happening to me? I need You!"

The more revelation I received, the more peace I had. As hunger for the Word increased, I had fewer symptoms and more energy to play with my kids, and joy and laughter returned to my house.

During this period, my family and I kept partaking of the holy Communion, sometimes five to six times a day, believing and declaring divine health in our bodies. I would partake of it whenever there were symptoms showing or if I had any weird thoughts. We also anointed ourselves with anointing oil and declared our healing. After five months, my symptoms got a whole lot better, but I still had my moments of crying and asking for more healing.

I listened to one of Pastor Prince's sermons where he preached about righteousness, and it spoke to me. I thought I had it down pat but God revealed to me that my understanding of His righteousness in Christ was still a bit shaky. It was then that I began searching for Pastor Prince's teachings on righteousness. I wanted to know what Jesus did for me and how much He loves me.

I began listening to Pastor Prince's sermons multiple times a day and more intensely. The more revelation I received, the more peace I had. As hunger for the Word increased, I had fewer symptoms and more energy to play with my kids, and joy and laughter returned to my house.

When I heard Pastor Prince preach on flowing with the Spirit and speaking in tongues, I began practicing this. When things got frustrating, I heard the Lord telling me to simply enjoy the day with Him. It felt restful and peaceful, and my little conversations with Him began to grow longer. I found that as I began to pray more and more in the Spirit, I went from a 65 to a 95 percent restoration of health within a few days!

I now know I am the righteousness of God in Christ, and the Holy Spirit lives in me, praying perfect prayers for me. Thank You, Abba Father!

Thank you, Pastor Prince. God bless you!

Melody | Kentucky, United States

Free from Depression and Suicidal Thoughts

I'd battled depression on and off over the years, but 2020 was the darkest time I've ever had. I felt like I was drowning in a ferocious storm as wave after wave tossed me around. On top of the effects of the global pandemic then and being isolated from the people I loved, I was getting hit by one negative situation after another. Eventually, I felt my heart completely shatter.

I sank into a deep depression. Overwhelming pain haunted me, leading me to beg the Lord for death. For four whole months, I cried every single day, sometimes multiple times a day. I found it difficult to get out of bed to shower, eat, or brush my teeth. Somehow, I still managed to get up and go to work every day although I really didn't see any point in doing that. I just wanted the pain to end. It felt like my mind was deteriorating and I was dying.

I don't really know when things changed for me specifically, but I know that six months later, I began reading Pastor Prince's book *Give Me This Mountain.*

At first, I found it really difficult to believe what God was saying about who I am and to see that His promises are true for me personally. As I continued to stick it out and kept reading the book, my mind started to change.

The more I saw Jesus, the more the wrong beliefs I didn't even know I had started falling off. I am so ecstatic to share that today, not only am I no longer depressed, but I am also filled with joy!

I began to see more and more of my Father's heart of love and compassion toward me and my situation. I felt Him loving me into wholeness. The Lord began restoring relationships I thought were too far gone to be salvaged. He also blessed me and gave me favor at work when I least deserved it. He was showing me that He is trustworthy and nothing is impossible for Him!

Suddenly, I found myself claiming every promise I read in Scripture and declaring them over my situations, believing the Lord paid for my peace of mind and healing in my heart and emotions by dying on the cross. The more I saw Jesus, the more the wrong beliefs I didn't even know I had started falling off.

I am so ecstatic to share that today, not only am I no longer depressed, but I am also filled with joy! The more I hear about how completely forgiven I am and that I am the righteousness of God in Christ not by my performance or obedience, the more the weight and pressure just melt off effortlessly. Now I am constantly hungry to hear more about Jesus! I'm also truly blessed to be a part of Grace Revolution Church in Texas. Praise the Lord. Thank You, Jesus!

Dana | Texas, United States

Special Appreciation

Special thanks and appreciation to all who have sent in their testimonies and praise reports to us. Kindly note that all testimonies are received in good faith and have been shared only with the consent of the testimony writers. Each testimony has been edited only for brevity and fluency. Names have been changed to protect the writers' privacy.

Medical Disclaimer

If you are facing a physical or mental health condition, please understand that this book is not meant to take the place of professional medical advice. If you or your loved one has a health concern or an existing medical condition, please do consult a qualified medical practitioner or healthcare provider. We would also advise you to ask and seek the Lord always for His wisdom and guidance regarding your specific health or medical issue and to exercise faith together with godly wisdom in the management of your own physical, mental, and emotional well-being. Do not, on your own accord, disregard any professional medical advice or diagnosis. Please also do not take what has been shared in this book as permission or encouragement to stop taking your medication or going for medical treatment. While we make no guarantees and recognize that different individuals experience different results, we continue to stand in faith to believe and affirm the authority and power of God's Word and healing promises with all who believe in the finished work that our Lord Jesus has accomplished on the cross.

Salvation Prayer

If you would like to receive all that Jesus has done for you and make Him your Lord and Savior, please pray this prayer:

> *Lord Jesus, thank You for loving me and dying for me on the cross. Your precious blood washes me clean of every sin. You are my Lord and my Savior, now and forever. I believe You rose from the dead and that You are alive today. Because of Your finished work, I am now a beloved child of God and heaven is my home. Thank You for giving me eternal life and filling my heart with Your peace and joy. Amen.*

We Would Like to Hear from You

If you have prayed the salvation prayer or if you have a testimony to share after reading this book, please let us know via GospelPartner.com/testimony.

Stay Connected with Joseph

Connect with Joseph through these social media channels and receive daily inspirational teachings:

Facebook.com/JosephPrince
Twitter.com/JosephPrince
YouTube.com/@JosephPrince
Instagram: @JosephPrince

Free Daily Devotional

Download the Joseph Prince app and access the free Daily Devotional and other resources. Available for iOS and Android devices. Visit GospelPartner.com/app.

Books by Joseph Prince

Live the Let-Go Life

Live the Let-Go Life is the go-to resource for anyone who wants to find freedom from the stress and anxieties of modern living. Instead of letting stress and all its negative effects rule your life, discover how you can cast all your cares on the One who cares about you like no other and experience His practical supply for every need. You'll find simple yet powerful truths and tools to help you get rid of worry and anxiety and experience greater health and well-being. Learn how you can tune in to God's peace, walk daily in His unforced rhythm of grace, and find yourself living healthier, happier, and having time for the important things in life!

Unstoppable Faith

Unstoppable Faith—31 Thoughts for Owning Your Portion brings you simple yet powerful thoughts on faith, one for each day of the month. Each thought in this pocket-size resource is accompanied by an encouraging scripture and bite-size devotional reading that will help you take small steps of faith daily. When you're feeling low on faith, this book will turn your eyes away from yourself and fix them on Jesus and His grace. Beautifully designed and filled with inspirational images, *Unstoppable Faith* will help you bask in the Lord's love for you as you trust Him for the turnarounds you need in your life.

No More Mind Games

Are you battling overwhelming discouragement today? Feel imprisoned by depression and crippling, defeatist thoughts? Discover in *No More Mind Games* how you are not alone, not without help, and why you can come out of the valley stronger. Get practical keys to help you break free from depression and anxiety and learn truths that will impart strength and hope to you. Come to know a Savior who is your very present help, who comes to you in the midst of your storm. The battle is the Lord's, and your victory is found in Him!

About the Author

JOSEPH PRINCE is a leading voice in proclaiming the gospel of grace to a whole new generation of believers and leaders. He is the senior pastor of New Creation Church in Singapore, a vibrant and dynamic church with a congregation of more than 33,000 attendees. He separately heads Joseph Prince Ministries, a television and media broadcast ministry that is reaching the world with the good news about the Lord Jesus' finished work. Joseph is also the bestselling author of *The Power of Right Believing* and *Destined to Reign* and a highly sought-after conference speaker. For more information about his other inspiring resources and his latest audio and video messages, visit JosephPrince.com.